Days of Sun

poems by

Susan Oleferuk

Finishing Line Press
Georgetown, Kentucky

Days of Sun

Copyright © 2017 by Susan Oleferuk
ISBN 978-1-63534-236-9 First Edition
All rights reserved under International and Pan-American Copyright Conventions.
No part of this book may be reproduced in any manner whatsoever without written permission from the publisher, except in the case of brief quotations embodied in critical articles and reviews.

ACKNOWLEDGMENTS

"Adventure." *The Avocet*. Fall. (2015):11. Print.
"Days of Sun." *Lone Star Magazine*. 82. (2016). Print.
"Days of Sun." *The Deronda Review*. 6.1 (2015): 3 Web.
"Days of Sun." *The Weekly Avocet*. 75 May (2014). Web.
"Decide." *The Deronda Review*. 6.2 (2016): 10. Web.
"Earth vs Man." *The Weekly Avocet*. 139 July (2015). Web
"From Cape Cod." *The Deronda Review*. 7.1 (2017): 25. Print.
"Ghost Town." *The Deronda Review*. 6.1 (2015): 3 Web.
"Iconography." *The Weekly Avocet*. 157 Dec. (2015). Web.
"If You Miss Me." *The Deronda Review*. 6.1 (2015): 13. Web.
"If You Miss Me". *The Weekly Avocet*. 104 Dec. (2014). Web.
"I Will Always Come to You in May." *The Deronda Review*. 7.1 (2017): 26. Print.
"I Will Always Come to You in May." *The Avocet*. Spring. (2017): 60. Print.
"Lover of Summer." *The Deronda Review*. 6.2 (2016): 4. Web.
"Refugees." *The Deronda Review*. 6.2 (2016): 5. Web.
"River." *The Weekly Avocet*. 178. May (2016). Web.
"Sizes and Shapes." *The Deronda Review*. 6.1 (2015): 8. Web.
"Soft Lines." *The Weekly Avocet*. 212. Jan. (2017). Web.
"Soft Lines." *The Deronda Review*. 7.1 (2017): 41. Print.
"The Hour of the Wolf." *The Weekly Avocet*. 170. Mar (2016). Web.
"The Larkspur." *The Weekly Avocet*. 188. July (2016). Web.
"The Larkspur." *The Deronda Review*. 7.1 (2017): 30. Print.
"The Trade." *The Deronda Review*. 6.2 (2016): 11. Web.
"The Woodland." *The Weekly Avocet*. 132. June (2015). Web.
"When the Eagle Flies." *The Weekly Avocet*. 235. June (2017). Web.
"Where the Sky Can See Us." *The Weekly Avocet*. 171. Mar (2016). Web.
"Winter Nights." *The Deronda Review*. 6.1 (2015) :4. Web.
"Winter Nights." *The Avocet*. 58 (2014). Web.

Publisher: Leah Maines
Editor: Christen Kincaid
Cover Art: Barbara Marshall
Author Photo: Barbara Marshall

Printed in the USA on acid-free paper.
Order online: www.finishinglinepress.com
also available on amazon.com

Author inquiries and mail orders:
Finishing Line Press
P. O. Box 1626
Georgetown, Kentucky 40324
U. S. A.

Contents

Days of Sun 1
If You Miss Me 2
Adventure 3
From Cape Cod 4
Ghost Town 5
River 6
Where the Sky Can See Us 7
Winter Nights 8
The Woodland 9
Refugees 10
Earth vs Man 11
Shapes and Sizes 12
The Hour of the Wolf 13
The Larkspur 14
Lover of Summer 15
The Trade 16
I Will Always Come to You in May 17
Iconography 18
When the Eagle Flies 19
Decide 20
The Whys and Wherefores 21
Soft Lines 22

To my sister, Lynn, with love

Days of Sun

There will be a day
when a feather will fall like an arrow
from an unlikely sky
a day when the cicadas hum
and the clouds rise majestic

There will be days, yes there will
when the frost etches forgotten scars
and the snowflakes fall heavy, slow and sad

There will be days of the peony, the poppy and rose
sensuous, insensible and full
the heartbreak hidden in the seed

And a day of sweet grass, cut and drying in the sun
the ditch of chicory and flax
some time to spend on the side of the road
sitting beside a friend, a dog, a lover, a child
yes, some such days

If You Miss Me

If you miss me, see me standing on the hill
looking toward the river
I won't tell you what I'm watching
I know now
no woman will
If you remember, gather the apples for the deer
you know where and when
I have a heaven I see in my mind clear
it is climbing the hill in the fall
the path damp and gold
the sky I'll take though of any color
I was never one to look up
and I've mismatched much
so if you miss me search not in the heavenly sky
look for me instead amongst the trees
near the river
on the hill.

Adventure

The lure of an unpaved road
past rusted parts and tire marks
winding into sweet meadow wood
a call to gentle adventure

The dragonfly fairy and hummingbird dragon
St. George dancing with a cardinal and starling
sunflower princes smug and swaying
the moonflowers virginal and dry
the season dying on the vine

I too feel years whipped and broken
but I know the magic is hidden
in every tale
in every road
in every dying season.

From Cape Cod

If you live long enough
everyone you love will betray you
and you will forgive them
for the tides and marshes of age and love are sharp and hurting
and deep
and dying a relief
when the years too long
when the losses multiply and thoughts dim
but hold here fast
for the sky is blue and wind salty and fresh
and the sun is lighting the pine
early this snow covered morning.

Ghost Town

I found myself in a strange city
the streets too wide, too empty, too meaningless
I was confused
that I had to leave my home
unattached I stood, unsteady, no footing
miles of losses behind me like the crumbs that would never lead me to return

I watched the finch fly through her familiar trees
as I looked far for something to remind me of home
but the past is a sad whisper on deserted streets
ever out of reach
each corner a wrong turn.

River

The day looked like it had been scraped from the bottom of a pot
the gray unpalatable, a greasy remains no way to catch in a grasp
and shape into a day
my body a worn old coat
mind, a stranger reeling in a rant
but every rain washes you free
if you step out
and slide and slip and look up
and see what you need to see
and me
I needed to see the river
a line of silver filigree
I will always need the river.

Where the Sky Can See Us

There are many ways to die and many ways
to live
and without a no
without a yes
you are walking paced by a watch,
run by a road, far from the sun
locked away from the lovely moon dripping dreams of long ago

So walk with me
to a trail darkening and lined by hard lived pine
and rest in a clearing and whisper your love
shout your yes
fight your no
and we'll climb
to where the sky can see us.

Winter Nights

Sleep deep in winter night
in the silence of hard cold
drift into the womb of the earth
and espy the stars and moon
where every dog is a wolf
and man large legend
stepping across constellations
like lighted bridges
linking the lost, the gone, the forbidden
we are hunters of brighter seasons
but sleep down deep in winters night now
and read the signs hidden.

The Woodland

They call to me and I to them
when I have caught a wish on the wind
a dandelion head
a cottonwood catkin
They are always around the bend
a splash, a laugh, a mist, a hum,
a hymn, a bole, a hole
to another realm
who knows who lives in this forest.

Refugees

The weeds on the trail were tall and I accidently
fell into the herd
startled they were lined up big and summer old
staring at me
I knew my place and lowered my eyes and turned

They belonged in the woods, they belonged on the earth,
they belonged with Egyptian kohl eyes, African necks meant to
reach the free skies
and the warm brown of slim trees
in Northern summer

And I, I was running for my life
so lost
bulldozed
by the sounds and heavy steps of mankind.

Earth vs Man

You left
but some nights
we both look up at a ring cast away
You visited
a winter day when I wore no gracious snow
The leaves lay on me as they had fallen
like your sad memories too
In the thicket
winterberry shone
reminding me of drops of your bubbling blood which will come back to me
the sun gave us both benediction
the birds sang a solemn psalm
oh we see each other rarely
yet wedded we once were.

Shapes and Sizes

I live where
if I lose a little
I lose a lot
when I find a little
I find a world
hidden in the hollows of trees
beyond the bent paths of Indiangrass

I fear the fog
when the world is walled too small
and I bump into myself and bruise
yet in the mists
I sleep deeply in the blanket of the world
feeling the slight shifts
the steps of the seasons

Come sit with me and watch
the changing sizes of hidden worlds
but beware the shapeshifters of harmful intent
and know what I would rouse myself from dreamy sleep to protect
know the ground I stand on
and what I can't lose.

The Hour of the Wolf

My old dog who lived at my feet, every bed, every seat
spent her last evenings outside in the winter chill
watching the sunset and trees she knew so well
seemingly waiting patiently for a call

As I watched her from the window hurt to be cut off
from this private life of dogs, I shivered… the hour of the wolf
when they remember they can hear beyond the wind
and make ready to pad off, leaving human life a scared cold thing.

The Larkspur

All flowers live up to their names
an eponymous breed claiming colors, scent and heart
warriors with spears rising in the field
able to bring us to our knees
reminding us of forgotten dreams
those small hidden places like shadows
under the dark leaves
surrender written on the wings of a moth

I loved the larkspur before I had ever seen one
one word conjuring another world and
I lived in both
the wildflower meadow sits in the sun
a disdainful garden needing no man
weaving spells and humming the land
all we can offer is
the glorious names.

Lover of Summer

I have a summer afternoon off
how do I tell those concerned
that I want to dip into the stillness like a pool
touch the trembling of my Rose of Sharon
and a wayward plump bee under my chin
confused by my bright t-shirt glow

My neighbor's cat naps under the hemlocks
I didn't know
tree tops hustle importantly
sensing a season change
flowers are grown, the goldfinch and sunflower are one
and I have won a skirmish of love to be alone

I am a child of summer
once a mighty swimmer, never a splasher
but my arms were always open to the sky and sea
now like the cat I dream in dark green
lick the sun like a bee, warm myself in memory
and as a lover of summer, I dive into this afternoon.

The Trade

In the dream we lay together on the side of the road
my face against your still warm brown fur, eyes large and
anguished
our blood cooling together
I had been driving on a foggy night
my arm was across your ribs as I died, we, probably
the same size, whispered every night
covered with leaves and mud and snow
as we lay waiting to be sent where
we did not know
in my guilt and growing love
I traded you my soul
I would return as the deer

You warned me of the hunger, the hunting, the cull, the cold
but I thought of the days in the air and sun
the freedom I had felt only here and there
in turn you heard of all that awaited you
the bounty, food, warmth, power too
and when we were called we walked two by two
we walked off two deer.

I Will Always Come to You in May

I will always come to you in May
poppies for remembrance, roses for love
honeysuckle tangled ties of abundance now gone
the dead speak in color, scent and song
so much else is forgotten

See my shadow in a moonflower before summers end
when the nights are still warm
and the stars speak like old friends
they tell the others what was and shall come
and for you the serene evenings bring dreams of new love

I lie in winters dead in the cold ground of my icy bed
far from strength, my hopes, my dread
but if I had one moment to claim as mine
the end of May would be my time, when the sky darkens and tender trees sway
and I drive through the hills to you.

Iconography

The fingerprints left smudged in the sky
the stars all set to light the way home
bird song mathematical and true
a shifting text of horizon
waves and sines shaping sea and light
summer high and ripe
the empty sacs and seeds and tears
so many messages and tracks
I am a tracker, a watcher, a reader
I stand on the bluff over the river
and search always search for you.

When the Eagle Flies

When the eagle flies
not the horizontal osprey aligned
or dark hawk acry
no only the eagle white head wise
leaving the land
you stay and stand
even if you've stood for nothing before
and if you can't watch those gifted skies, then I can't explain
that little loneliness,
that shuddering loneliness of mine.

Decide

Where is the tree that stood on the hill
the mossy stone wall, a century strength
a small house below, window boxes and lace
the woman who loved it and left

The metals have been blowing with the anxious ashes of the dead
memories scattered like refugees
identities picked like pockets
stories opened from a can
there are many truths they say, many friends… none
I stand on my head and east is west

The big dipper feeds the earth
pours in the night and tucks us in
the north star an heirloom for when the streams run dry
yes it changes, we change, growth, destruction,
 raise your tired head to the wind and decide.

The Whys and Wherefores

A world of w's has been my lot
I think I shall put them in a biscuit box
where I keep my wishes, wisdom and whatnots
there they'll be among the crumbs I left
in their place I'll gather the letters of colors and scents
the shapes of leaves and the eyes of trees and I'll
arrange my new life like a Lego set
as I lie in my hammock in a chilly breeze
imagining I'm sailing rough seas
in a Roman trireme or Medieval caravel
only my left foot warmed by a Mediterranean sun
and if you ask me Where
I'll say I don't care
if you question Why
I'll no longer lie
I shall plunder the alphabet like a laughing sailor.

Soft Lines

The gray cloud folds back like a blanket to reveal a sleepy sun
it begins until it ends and the day is filled
with clouds, some stark but few straight lines
a fine fuzziness to amuse in fact
I cannot think when I have ever walked
a straight path
that didn't turn or curve or send me up another hill

So we can't sum up the day saying
Ah I went there when the going was so tumbled and strained
that you really landed
somewhere else
the back of the beyond, the back, the beyond, or somewhere near it
but night is folding on a soft black line
curved like a sweater dropped by the bed.

Susan Oleferuk is the author of *Circling for Home* and *Those Who Come to The Garden* also published by Finishing Line Press. She teaches in New York.

www.ingramcontent.com/pod-product-compliance
Lightning Source LLC
LaVergne TN
LVHW041521070426
835507LV00012B/1743